THE CHOSEN VESSEL

BY DYLAN VAN DEN BERG

AFTER THE SHORT STORY BY BARBARA BAYNTON

CURRENCY PRESS
The performing arts publisher

CURRENT THEATRE SERIES

First published in 2025
by Currency Press Pty Ltd,
Gadigal Land, Suite 310, 46–56 Kippax Street, Surry Hills, NSW 2010, Australia
enquiries@currency.com.au
www.currency.com.au

in association with The Street Theatre

Typeset by Brighton Gray for Currency Press.
Printed by Fineline Print + Copy Services, Revesby, NSW.
Cover image by Tobi Skerra for The Street Theatre.

Currency Press acknowledges the Traditional Owners of the Country on which we live and work. We pay our respects to all Aboriginal and Torres Strait Islander Elders, past and present.

A catalogue record for this
book is available from the
National Library of Australia

Contents

This play was written and workshopped
on Ngunnawal and Ngambri Country.

I pay my respects to Ngunnawal and Ngambri Elders.

Always was, always will be—
Aboriginal Land.

The moonlight on the gleaming clay was a ‘heavenly light’ to him, and he knew the *white* figure not for flesh and blood, but for the Virgin and Child of his mother’s prayers.

Barbara Baynton, *The Chosen Vessel* (1902)

The Chosen Vessel was first performed at The Street Theatre, Ngunnawal and Ngambri country, Canberra, on 9 August 2025, with the following cast and creatives:

WOMAN	Laila Thaker
SWAGMAN	Craig Alexander

Director, Abbie-lee Lewis
Set Designer, Angie Matsinos
Costume Designer, Leah Ridley
Lighting Designer, Nathan Sciberras
Sound Designer, Kyle Sheedy

CHARACTERS

WOMAN. A young Aboriginal and/or Torres Strait Islander woman.

GHOST. The spirit of an Aboriginal and/or Torres Strait Islander woman.

SWAGMAN. A violent white man.

HUSBAND. A husband in name only. White man.

YOUNG MAN. A white, teenage boy who's kind to WOMAN (initially).

HORSEMAN. A young, naive white man.

BARMAN. The voice of a white man.

TRAVELLERS. A collection of white men, travelling.

PRIEST. An old white man who sees the truth but chooses to ignore it.

WOMAN and GHOST are played by one Aboriginal and Torres Strait Islander, woman-identifying actor. SWAGMAN, HUSBAND, YOUNG MAN, HORSEMAN, BARMAN, TRAVELLERS and PRIEST are played by one white, man-identifying actor.

SETTING

The early 1900s.

A small house in the middle of the bush. A whitefella house in town. A pub.

A spirit-world.

A NOTE ON STAGING

Consider what we see or don't see or can't know.

Scenes A, B, C, etc., are offers for moments of the chase between WOMAN and SWAGMAN.

This playtext went to press before the end of rehearsals and may differ from the play as performed.

SCENE ONE

The faint light of a hand-held lantern—

Moving closer closer closer.

Floorboards creaking.

Footsteps all around.

Leaves rustling.

Distant cries, too muffled to make out.

It's uncomfortable.

Almost like an arm could snake up from the ground and grab you by the ankle.

Then—

GHOST *appears.*

Maybe we don't see her at first.

Maybe she's somewhere we wouldn't expect.

She speaks directly to the audience.

GHOST: Shame about the dark, ain't it?

Used to be somethin' to look at. *Really* somethin'.

We had mountains that hummed with life. Down near the sea, you could taste the salt in the air. Flowers, pretty as anything you've ever seen. No fences or roads or towers or *order*—except for what Country laid out for us.

The trees didn't droop in grief. The grass didn't turn grey.

An eagle flyin' overhead woulda seen it for what it was—

The most peerless piece of earth the sun ever shone down on.

Same land you're sittin' on now—

Stolen land.

Easy to forget, eh?

Comfy in ya seat—

Wine dribblin' down ya chin.

Ah, to go back!

And the best thing of all?

Pause.

We had quiet.

Pause.

We got stories stamped on our skin, stretching up our arms and across our backs.

You heard 'em before?

Think you heard 'em.

But the truth's like a whisper, ain't it?

You hear it, and you think—

'Oh no!'

'How awful!'

You'd think our tales would cure deafness, wouldn't ya?

But here I am—

Dragged back to tell ya.

GHOST *places the lantern somewhere and light envelops her face.*

It goes like this.

A woman.

A baby who's not yet three months old.

A calf, tethered to the gate.

A house with a track running along the front.

TRAVELLER *appears.*

A few travellers passed along at intervals.

Most of 'em kept to themselves—horseman with business in town, ridin' in to vote or kiss their mothers. Some of 'em were young fellas puffed up with pride just 'cause they owned a hat and wiggled a worm between their legs—a worm they'd never used but spend every wakin' moment thinkin' about.

Then swagmen—

Going to, or coming from, the dismal, drunken little town—

TRAVELLER: A day's journey—

GHOST: They terrified her the most.

TRAVELLER: A house!

GHOST: A house! To call upon! To ask for—

TRAVELLER: Water?

Bread?

A place to rest my head?

GHOST: She'd never tell them the truth, of course.
That it's *her* and the *baby*—
That it's *them* and their *dreams*—
Dreams of gettin' home—
Of fillin' up the bag she keeps at the door—
And takin' on the hills—
And findin' her way back to her Country.
She'd never tell 'em that there's no man around no more, tethering her up like a calf to a post—
TRAVELLER: Ya husband here?
GHOST: [*as* WOMAN] My husband—
Here.
Out the back.
Asleep.
[*As* GHOST] And they'd say—
TRAVELLER: This time of day? Man asleep? Must be—
GHOST: [*as* WOMAN] Sick.
TRAVELLER: Ah.
GHOST: And so he'd leave.
And months would go by—
Until—
TRAVELLER: Water?
Bread?
A place to rest my head?
GHOST: Deep breath.
[*As* WOMAN] Husband out the back—
Sick—
Here—
But asleep—
TRAVELLER: Water?
GHOST: [*as* WOMAN] Here—
TRAVELLER: Bread?
GHOST: [*as* WOMAN] Only a little—
TRAVELLER: A place to rest my head—
GHOST: [*as* WOMAN] River's down that way—
TRAVELLER: I'll be on my way—
GHOST: And then another—

TRAVELLER: Water?
GHOST: [*as* WOMAN] Here —
TRAVELLER: Bread?
GHOST: [*as* WOMAN] Yes—
TRAVELLER: A place to—
GHOST: [*as* WOMAN] The river—
TRAVELLER: Most grateful—
GHOST: And then the baby would cry.
Pierce through the whole thing.
TRAVELLER: Got a bit on your hands, eh, love?

Pause.

GHOST: The woman checked the bag almost every day—
Pulled the items out and checked 'em—
Counted 'em.
A blanket.
A knife.
The shells she got from her mother—
Who got 'em from *her* mother.
She'd make a plan—
She'd *resolve*—
To go.
But the days got in her way.
Too hot—
Baby's sick—
Food's gone bad—
Storm cloud brewin'—
To many blokes lurkin' in the dark who care nothin' for a black woman and her baby—
Who think only of a tingle at the end of their dick.

Pause.

Always a reason to stay.

The sounds of a baby crying.

And off this yarn goes.
The baby cries.
The woman waits.

Knowin'—
Hopin'—
The day will come.

[*A*]

A gasp.

A scream.

Darkness closing in on WOMAN, *clutching her baby.*

It's like the shadow of a hundred hands are coming at her from every direction.

The thud of metal on wood.

There's only a tiny column of light untainted by the black.

WOMAN *squeezes herself and baby into it.*

A heartbeat races.

And then—

Darkness.

SCENE TWO

A baby cries.

GHOST *makes her way towards a cradle.*

GHOST *looks at baby.*

There's a moment of deep sorrow.

As GHOST *picks up baby—*

She becomes WOMAN.

None of the assuredness of GHOST.

She's young.

More scared of motherhood than being alone.

She tries to settle the crying baby.

WOMAN: Sssssshhhhh.
Ssshhhhhhh.
Hush—

Hush now—

She frantically moves around the space, trying to comfort her child.

Sleep now.

More crying.

Time to sleep.
Shhhhh.
Please.
Hush.
Hush!

WOMAN *begins humming a tune.*

Baby cries.

WOMAN *hums louder.*

And louder.

Baby doesn't stop.

Just—
STOP!

WOMAN *places baby back in the cradle.*

It might be rough. It might surprise her.

She slides to the floor.

She weeps silently.

Baby's cries subside.

WOMAN *freezes.*

Too good to be true?

My mother—a good mother—a mother with a soft neck and gentle hands—told me stories till my eyes got heavy.
But I don't—
I don't have—

Pause.

I carried you around in my belly, you know?
Slept on my side, sweat through the night, ache in my back.

My hands grew old while you grew big.
What do you think about? When you sleep?
Milk? My breasts? My face?

Pause.

Wonder what *he* looks like?
Your father. *A* father.

You look round the room like you know something's missing, like you know it took more than just *me* to make you, like you should have more than just me to love you.

Only saw him once, 'fore he slammed a door on us, threat of his knife always there, clinging to his waist.

Now I gotta love you enough for two people.
Two whole people.
And I—

Baby stirs.

If I could talk to you, it wouldn't be like this.
Could talk you out of sadness.
When you're older—

WOMAN *looks away from baby.*

Why do you look like him?
Came out of *me*, didn't you?
Had two sets of eyes to choose from—
Two sets of hands and feet—
Didn't have to choose those creases on your forehead, did you?
Didn't have to take on his nose—
Shape of his mouth—
Why'd you chose all of that?

Pause.

Got my hair.
Not much of it but can tell it's mine.
Gonna grow it long so it'll cover up everything that isn't me—
That isn't mine—
Will cover your whole face and your whole body—
Hair down to your ankles.
And I'll brush it every day, so it won't trouble you.

Baby stirs again.

WOMAN *whispers.*

Please sleep please sleep please sleep please sleep please sleep please sleep PLEASE SLEEP PLEASE SLEEP.

You gotta be tired. Rest. Rest now before you can't lay down without a pain somewhere—'cross your ribs, down your legs, lump in your neck caught there like a plum seed stuck in your throat. Pain in your head, too, needles in your brain every time you shut your eyes, and only three things ever look clear—ever look like they should—your mother's face, the tree where you were born, leaves brown and green and—

His face—

'Cause he forced your eyes open with his fat fingers, made you look straight at him.

Those are the only things you can conjure up in your brain. Like everything else got sucked right out by time or by god or maybe you just not too smart to start with.

So rest *now*.

While you can.

Baby is asleep.

That's my girl.

When you got more strength—

When I can face heading up that hill—

We'll get out of here.

I promise.

WOMAN *checks the contents of the bag.*

She picks out a blanket, a knife, a shell necklace.

There's a sort of ritual to it.

For the cold—

For cutting through the scrub—

For—

Suddenly—

A disturbance from outside.

The braying of a calf.

WOMAN *panics.*

No no no no no no no—
Not now, my darling—
Baby's just down.
Baby's asleep.

The calf has a leash, which WOMAN *gently tugs.*

Just a baby yourself, aren't ya?
Sweet thing, aren't ya, girl?
What's out there, eh?
Dogs?
Looking for your mother?

WOMAN *looks into the distance.*

Better get you tied up.

The calf bleats.

Sssshhhh.
I know. I'm sorry.
Calf needs a feed as much as a baby.
Got no milk or stories.
Got nothin' but a stroke for ya head.

WOMAN *slides to the ground, leaning on the calf.*

She clutches the bag.

[***B***]

SWAGMAN *appears, one arm groping in the darkness—*

The other gushing with blood.

SWAGMAN *snarls and shouts—*

He trips on the scrub and scrabbles along a riverbank on his belly.

He stops.

He listens.

He hears something and snakes out an arm—

His eyes light up—

He laughs from deep in his chest.

He speaks almost in a whisper.

SWAGMAN: Got ya!

SCENE THREE

The kitchen of a whitefella house. It's big.

GHOST *appears.*

GHOST: Before she was a mother—
She was a girl.
Slipped from one home—
One family—
Into another—
And made to work.

GHOST *becomes* WOMAN.

WOMAN *is young.*

Seven or eight years old.

She's mopping the floor.

A YOUNG MAN *appears.*

He's the same age. He's awkward.

YOUNG MAN: Oh.
Sorry—
I didn't mean to—
WOMAN: It's fine.
I'll be done soon.

YOUNG MAN *tries to walk across the mopped floor.*

I just mopped that—
Can you go a different way?
Please.
Sir.
YOUNG MAN: Oh.
Yes.
I'm sorry—
I didn't—
I'll go this way—

YOUNG MAN *moves off in another direction but slips on the wet floor.*

Arrrghhhh!
I'm sorry I'm sorry I'm sorry—

WOMAN: Ya 'right?

YOUNG MAN: I'm—
I'm fine—
It's these boots—
They've got a flat sole—
Nothing to cling to the dirt let alone floorboards—
Let alone *wet* floorboards—
I'm fine.
Really fine.

YOUNG MAN *awkwardly gets up.*

He tries to move carefully across the mopped floor.

WOMAN: Too much water and soap.

YOUNG MAN: Sorry?

WOMAN: I used too much water and soap.

YOUNG MAN: It's fine—
It was my own—

WOMAN: Do you want me to—
I can tell them.
I can do it myself.

YOUNG MAN: Tell who?

WOMAN: Your parents.
Your mother.

YOUNG MAN: No—
No no no no no—
It was me—
It was my fault—

WOMAN: Your mother said to make it shine.

YOUNG MAN: She could do it herself if she cares that much.

Pause.

Is there anywhere around here—
To ummm—
Hide?

WOMAN: That cupboard.
No-one looks in there.

YOUNG MAN *moves towards the cupboard and almost slips again.*

YOUNG MAN: Shit!
WOMAN: Don't walk on your toes.
That might help.
YOUNG MAN: Ah.
Yes.
Got it.

Pause.

Coming?

YOUNG MAN *gestures to the cupboard.*

WOMAN: Oh.
Nah.
I've got stuff to do—
YOUNG MAN: Just for a moment.
Can show you something.

WOMAN *and* YOUNG MAN *awkwardly climb into the cupboard and close the door.*

I took these.

YOUNG MAN *has a jar of rock candy.*

Wanna try?
WOMAN: What is it?
YOUNG MAN: You don't—?
They're sweets.

WOMAN *shrugs.*

They're sweet.
And they sit in your mouth and they make everything better.
You kind of suck on them?
And the sweet stays in your mouth for—
Ages.
A long time.
They're my father's.

WOMAN: I've never—
Had one.
YOUNG MAN: Well.
This is good news for your gob.
Because you are about to be taken to another place—
You're about to transform—
WOMAN: All from a little red rock?
YOUNG MAN: You'll see.

YOUNG MAN *gives* WOMAN *a piece of rock candy.*

Ready?
WOMAN: I think?
YOUNG MAN: Let's do it.

They both put the rock candy in their mouths.

WOMAN *is unsure for a moment.*

WOMAN: What is this—
It's—
Oh.
Ohhhh.
Ohhhhhh.
YOUNG MAN: Told you.
WOMAN: Still waiting to transform.
But pretty nice.
YOUNG MAN: My father never lets me have them.
'Eat a peach instead!'
But nothing that grows on a tree can taste like that.
WOMAN: It can.
There are berries—
That taste like this—
Like—
It's different—
But the same.
YOUNG MAN: Never had them before.
WOMAN: Grow all around here.
Can cook them.
Or eat them as they come.

YOUNG MAN: I'd like to try one.
WOMAN: I can—
    I can bring you some.
YOUNG MAN: That'd be—
    Nice.

Pause.

Another one?
WOMAN: Another one.

They eat more sweets.

YOUNG MAN *speaks with his mouth full.*

YOUNG MAN: Close your eyes—
    Don't chew it—
    Just let it sit there.
    What does it make you think about?

WOMAN *speaks with her mouth full.*

WOMAN: I should get back to the floors—
YOUNG MAN: Close your eyes—
    Come on—
WOMAN: I dunno—
YOUNG MAN: Okay—
    I'll go first.

YOUNG MAN *closes his eyes and concentrates.*

Makes me think about …
    Ridin' into town—
    On a horse—
    Like—
    A *proper* horse—
WOMAN: You ever been on one?
YOUNG MAN: Nah—
    Not yet.
    But I will.
    I'll ride into town, real slow.
    No wavin' or nothin'.
    Just me and the horse and everyone is gonna stop and look.

And they'll say—
They'll say—
'There he is.'
WOMAN: That's … nice.
YOUNG MAN: Now you.

Pause.

WOMAN: I'm thinking about a river—
And getting my feet wet.
I'm thinking about a fire on one side of me—
And my mother on the other side.
And the night-time above—
Counting stars till my eyes go blurry.

Pause.

YOUNG MAN: Maybe I could come to the river—
WOMAN: On your horse?
YOUNG MAN: On my horse.
We could eat sweets till our teeth fall out.
WOMAN: We could—

A muffled yell from somewhere in the house.

YOUNG MAN: Shit shit shit.
Ssssssshhh.
Don't move.
Don't—

The cupboard door opens and light streams in.

WOMAN *and* YOUNG MAN *are terrified.*

The strangled yell of a grown man.

YOUNG MAN *is dragged away.*

WOMAN *becomes* GHOST.

GHOST: She stayed a few years.
Got older and stronger and smarter.
Learned how to make herself invisible when the man of the house came callin' or his wife started hollerin' down the hall.
Learned how to sneak moments with the boy.
They don't stay kids for long—

Two shadows in a quiet house—
Sproutin' dreams with sugar on their tongues.

Pause.

Like water wearin' down a stone—
Change don't come all at once.

SCENE FOUR

The kitchen in a whitefella home.

WOMAN *is a bit older now. Fourteen or fifteen.*

She cleans pots and pans.

Suddenly—

YOUNG MAN—*also fourteen or fifteen—appears from behind the kitchen table.*

YOUNG MAN: AYYYYYYYEEEEEEEE!

WOMAN *screams and drops several pots.*

They clang.

Ha—
Scared ya—
Ha—

WOMAN *starts to cry.*

She looks to the ceiling and listens.

What?
It's just—
Just a joke.
Just trying to—
Surprise—

WOMAN: You better get goin'.

YOUNG MAN: No—
I'm—

WOMAN: Told to be quiet down here—
Told not to make a noise.
Your mother said so.

WOMAN *starts to clean up the pots.*

YOUNG MAN: I thought it would be funny.
WOMAN: Did ya?
Maybe think harder next time.
YOUNG MAN: Whoa.
Okay.
That how it is?
WOMAN: It is.
Yeah.

Pause.

YOUNG MAN: I'm not even allowed down here.
Not even allowed to talk to—
But I came—
To make a joke.

Pause.

You think I'm so—
Un-funny?

Pause.

WOMAN: You been funnier.
YOUNG MAN: Oh yeah?
WOMAN: Yeaaaaaah.
YOUNG MAN: Like when?
WOMAN: When you put burning sticks in your hair—
Pretendin' to be a tree on fire—
That's funny.

YOUNG MAN *acts it out.*

YOUNG MAN: Arrrghhh—
Help!
Think of the birds!

WOMAN *smiles slightly, wiping away tears.*

Still not funny enough?
WOMAN: You got no sticks or flames in ya hair.

Pause.

YOUNG MAN: What about this then?

YOUNG MAN *grabs a pile of clean pots, stacked atop one another.*

WOMAN: Nah—
Put 'em down.
YOUNG MAN: I could.

He holds them menacingly over the timber floor.

WOMAN: DON'T—
I mean—
Please—
Just leave—
Leave them—
I didn't mean—
YOUNG MAN: Laugh and I'll stop.
WOMAN: What?
YOUNG MAN: Laugh—
And I'll put 'em down—
WOMAN: You serious?

YOUNG MAN *shrugs.*

YOUNG MAN: No clangin' if you laugh.
WOMAN: No—
I can't just—

YOUNG MAN *pretends to drop the pots.*

NO!
YOUNG MAN: Then laugh.

WOMAN *stares at* YOUNG MAN.

YOUNG MAN *stares at* WOMAN.

WOMAN: Ha.
Ha ha ha ha ha—

WOMAN *tries to laugh convincingly.*

Hahahahaha—
Hahahahahahahaha—
YOUNG MAN: More—

WOMAN *holds her belly and laughs like a court jester—*

It comes from somewhere deep in her body.

WOMAN: HahahahahahaHAHAHAHAHAHAhahahahaHAHAHA.
HAHAHAHAH—

YOUNG MAN: Enough now—
Stop—

WOMAN: HAHAHAHAHAHA—

YOUNG MAN: Stop stop stop—
I'll put 'em down—

WOMAN*'s laughter becomes a sob.*

Okay okay okay okay okay—
I'm sorry—
Was just a—
Yeah.

WOMAN *slides to the floor and covers her face.*

I'll see ya later on.
Yeah?
Bring me those berries—
Yeah?
We can—
Have 'em together.

Pause.

Yeah?

WOMAN *is silent.*

YOUNG MAN *leaves.*

WOMAN *stands up and approaches the pile of pots.*

She considers them for a moment—

Then launches them off the table and onto the floor.

The muffled sounds of a woman's voice can be heard overhead—

Rageful.

WOMAN *becomes* GHOST.

GHOST: She never saw the boy again—
Lost the job—
Kicked out on her arse.

Made a plan to get back home—
To get her feet wet.
But where's home, eh?
When you been dragged away from it—
Turned round on your head a hundred times?

Pause.

The way home closed off before she got there.
Someone else came round—
Not a boy—
But a man—
A *husband*—
Smilin'—
Promisin'—
Askin' for her like she had a choice in the matter.

Pause.

The plan got folded away.

[***C***]

WOMAN *tears through the bush.*

She clings to her baby.

She drops to the ground, crawling along the riverbank, calculating each scrape of her knees through the low-lying scrub.

She stops and listens.

Silence.

And then—

She's jolted by a tug on her leg.

She doesn't scream or gasp—

She grunts.

She reaches around and her fingers find a thick branch.

She swings it over her head several times—

Stabbing, whacking, shoving—

Until she's free.

She scrambles to her feet, clinging to the branch.

It drips with blood.

She hurls it into the night and runs.

SCENE FIVE

WOMAN *is pregnant.*

HUSBAND *kneels in front of her swollen belly.*

HUSBAND: I can see through ya belly.
Through ya skin.
And I see a foot—
A perfect foot.
WOMAN: If you reckon—
HUSBAND: Boy's foot.
WOMAN: How do you figure that?
HUSBAND: Always end up with boys in my family.
Only girls we've got are the mothers—
Married in—
And they spit out more boys, who make mothers of more girls and it goes on and on like that.
WOMAN: First time for all things, ain't there?

Pause.

HUSBAND: Will give him a good strong name.
Grow him up big.
Grow him up smart—but not too much.
Smart men don't like workin' hard.
Brains get too big for shearin'.
WOMAN: I'll give her a name that means something.
And I'll grow her up strong, too.
And she'll be smart.
Smarter than most.
And she'll run faster than anyone.
And she'll be the right amount of me.

Pause.

HUSBAND: Think that all ya want.
But I'm tellin' ya—there's a boy cookin' away in there.
And for the kid's sake—
Got a better chance as half-caste man than woman.
And that's just the facts.

HUSBAND *disappears.*

WOMAN *becomes* GHOST.

GHOST: His words hung heavy on her brain.
She'd feel a flicker in her belly—
Like a fish turnin' in water—
And think *maybe …*
When his voice got sharp—
She'd think about sayin' goodbye—
About seekin' help to snuff out the new life inside.
She knew what this place could do to a child born half hers—
Half his.
Would the baby know her own mother from lookin'?

[***D***]

Thunder and lightning and a racing heartbeat.

WOMAN, *clutching baby to her chest, wades through the river.*

It becomes more frenetic—

Or maybe it gets slower—

Contradicting the storm and the racing heart.

WOMAN *stops.*

She looks this way—

Then that way—

She climbs up the bank of the river.

Her foot gets caught in the root of a tree.

SWAGMAN *reaches for her, panting and exhausted.*

WOMAN *kicks him in the face, and he slides into the river.*

WOMAN *and baby disappear.*

SCENE SIX

WOMAN *appears at the back entrance to a pub.*

She's disguised herself in some way.

She knocks on the door.

We hear the voice of a BARMAN.

BARMAN: Can I help ya?
WOMAN: I'm looking for …
A woman.
BARMAN: Who?
WOMAN: I'm not—
BARMAN: Need a name.
WOMAN: I don't have one—
Just told to—
Ask to see a woman.

Pause.

BARMAN: Wait here.

BARMAN *slams the door closed.*

Silence.

WOMAN *clutches her stomach.*

Almost willing something to happen.

She looks to the sky.

She looks to the ground.

And then—

A PRIEST *appears.*

PRIEST: Come out of the cold, love.

WOMAN *is startled.*

WOMAN: Oh.
They said there'd be a—
A woman.
I'm here to see a woman.

PRIEST: What you're after—
There's no woman willing.
What's on your mind?

WOMAN: My—
Mind?

Pause.

Home.

Home's where there's a bunch of arms to place your baby, mother's arms, arms of mothers who've been mothers to more than just their own, arms that've brought sleep and comfort and warmth.

Without home—
I don't know if—
I can't—

WOMAN *holds her belly.*

PRIEST: You've got a new home now.
And if you do what's on your mind—
If you move against the will of God—
He will make sure—
And I will make sure—
And any man blessed with the fear of God will make sure—
You never see home again.

PRIEST *disappears.*

WOMAN *becomes* GHOST.

GHOST: A baby can become love—can slip into something you never imagined—can help get you closer to home.

The woman runs.
Not away—
But towards—
Whatever comes next.

The swell of a baby's cry.

SCENE SEVEN

GHOST *sits next to baby's cradle.*

HUSBAND *eats his dinner.*

GHOST: He start off like—
HUSBAND: Good baby, we got, eh sweetheart?
GHOST: Her husband's got a habit of eatin' with his mouth filled up.
HUSBAND: We got a good baby, don't we?
GHOST: Her husband's got a habit of sayin' the same thing twice.
HUSBAND: Off to shearin' come springtime.
GHOST: Shoves food in his gob—
HUSBAND: Off to shearin'.
GHOST: Smiles at her and the baby.
HUSBAND: Gonna miss ya.
GHOST: Charred meat stuck in his teeth.
HUSBAND: Gonna miss you two, ain't I?
GHOST: She won't notice he's gone.
HUSBAND: Headin' for a smoke.
GHOST: Husband gets up, scrapin' his chair on the boards.
Scrapin' wakes the baby—
Baby who just gone to sleep.
She tells him—
'Mindful of the baby, please.'

GHOST *becomes* WOMAN.

HUSBAND: Eh?
WOMAN: The baby—she's—
HUSBAND: What? Eh? The baby's what?
WOMAN: Crying—
She's—
HUSBAND: Crying because of me?
WOMAN: No—
HUSBAND: Shut it up.
WOMAN: I'm trying—
HUSBAND: Shut it up—

Shut that baby up—
Stop that fucking noise—
Make it stop—
SHUT.
THAT.
BABY.
UP.

HUSBAND *raises his hand towards* WOMAN.

WOMAN *turns back into* GHOST.

GHOST *grabs* HUSBAND*'s arm and prevents his strike.*

They're in an arm wrestle.

GHOST: Got a fist like a wet fish, don't ya?
Got a brain smaller than a pebble.
Got a dick like a dead worm.
Got no feelin' for ya wife or ya baby.
Got no family to come back to, come springtime.
Ya wife'll be gone, takin' the baby.
HUSBAND: Got ten black women who'd kill to take your spot—
GHOST: For a bite of bread and a lick of water?
Kill to sit round your table?
Lay in your bed?
Got ten black women who'd kill to go home—
Kill to forget—
Kill to see Country—
Kill to put their feet in the river—
Kill to never see ya face—
Ever.
Again.

GHOST *wins the arm wrestle.*

HUSBAND *disappears.*

SCENE EIGHT

A house in the bush.

GHOST *rocks baby.*

GHOST: He left one morning before the sun came up.
Didn't say nothin'.
Just the sound of boots in the dirt.
She had the house—
Just her, the baby, the calf she took in like a lodger, feedin' it scraps.
Calf never raised its voice—
Never spat words across the room.
Just blinked slow.
Didn't bother her like them travellers comin' past—

TRAVELLER *appears.*

TRAVELLER: Water?
Bread?
A place to rest my head?
GHOST: She attended to their needs—
A good woman—
While the plan rolled around in her head—
TRAVELLER: Water?
GHOST: [*as* WOMAN] Baby gotta get strong—
TRAVELLER: Bread?
GHOST: [*as* WOMAN] Food enough for three day's walk—
TRAVELLER: A place to rest my head?
GHOST: [*as* WOMAN] A shield from the cold—
TRAVELLER: Sorry to trouble ya, love.

Pause.

GHOST: And it was in the early morning—
When she lay listening to her baby breathe—
That she heard somethin' better than music.

GHOST *becomes* WOMAN.

Baby starts to giggle.

WOMAN: What's that, my girl?

Baby giggles again.

What's that, eh?
Something funny, eh?

WOMAN *smiles, too.*

Like a little bird, aren't ya?

WOMAN *and baby giggle together.*

We'll go soon.
You and me.
That's right!
Tomorrow.
Tomorrow.
Tomorrow we go home.

The sun starts to come up.

WOMAN *and baby bask in its glow.*

SCENE NINE

WOMAN *gently rocks baby to sleep.*

No crying, no fuss.

Then—

A knock.

A voice.

WOMAN: Yes?

Pause.

SWAGMAN: Just a lost bloke, love.
WOMAN: Where you headed?
SWAGMAN: Town, I suppose—
WOMAN: Follow the river—
SWAGMAN: The river?
WOMAN: Takes you straight to town.
SWAGMAN: You know your way around, eh?

Wouldn't want to give you any trouble, love, but you got a cup of water?

WOMAN: Water?

SWAGMAN: Thirsty work, walkin'.

WOMAN: I don't—

SWAGMAN: Just an old man and his dog.

Pause.

WOMAN: Your dog?

SWAGMAN: That's it.
Been together since he was a pup.

WOMAN: You've been past here before?

SWAGMAN: From time to time.

WOMAN: And you don't know your way.

SWAGMAN: Know my way to the river. I get my water from there, drag it back up the hill to where I'm campin'.
Votin' happening. Got to get into town.

WOMAN: Oh.

SWAGMAN: Not somethin' that burdens you, I imagine, love.

Pause.

WOMAN: No.

SWAGMAN: I'll be on my way.
Appreciate the directions—
And appreciate that water, if you've got some handy.

Pause.

WOMAN: What's his name?

SWAGMAN: Eh?

WOMAN: The dog.

SWAGMAN: Call him Smudge.
Found him playin' round in an old fire.
Charcoal all through his fur.
Big bit across his face.
So he's called Smudge.

WOMAN: He likes you.

SWAGMAN: Never seen a more devoted match than me and him.

Pause.

Dragged me outta a ditch by my sleeves, once.
Had a couple of—
You know—
A drink—
And fell like a brick shit-house—
Pardon my language—
Straight into a hole.
Was pourin' with rain, you see—
Hole was fillin' up, you see—
And with a couple of drinks on board—
Who knows what mighta happened.
You see?

SWAGMAN *becomes tearful.*

Old boy saved me from drownin' in the muck.

Pause.

WOMAN: Loyal.
You're lucky.

WOMAN *pours* SWAGMAN *some water.*

SWAGMAN *downs it in one go.*

SWAGMAN: Go on—don't be shy.

WOMAN *pours another.*

And for my little fella too?

SWAGMAN *indicates a dog outside.*

WOMAN: I don't have anything to—
SWAGMAN: How 'bout that bowl?
Usin' it for somethin'?

WOMAN *pours water into the bowl.*

Be a love, would ya?

SWAGMAN *points outside.*

Can barely feel my feet.

WOMAN *hesitates.*

She doesn't want to leave baby.

Don't keep the poor bastard waiting.

WOMAN *quickly takes the water outside.*

She rushes back.

Bit of hurry about ya.
I like that.

WOMAN: I'd better be getting on with things.
My husband—

SWAGMAN: Husband?

WOMAN: Yes.
He's—
Unwell.
Sleeping just through here. Best not to wake him.

SWAGMAN: Come down with somethin', has he?

WOMAN: All the shearers—whole lot of them—came down with it.

SWAGMAN: Sorry to hear it.

WOMAN: Between him and the baby, there's a lot for me to—

SWAGMAN: I hear ya, love.
Don't you lot have *ways*? You know, healin' spells or somethin'?

WOMAN: Don't know what you're sayin'—

SWAGMAN: Blackfellas. You got potions and stuff to help—

WOMAN: We got knowledge.
But we still get sick, same as you lot.

SWAGMAN: Is that so?

Pause.

So, your husband—

WOMAN: A whitefella.

SWAGMAN: Ah.
We're both lucky then, ain't we?
Me with my dog.
You with your whitefella husband.

WOMAN: If you say so.

SWAGMAN: But could I trouble you for something to tide over my belly?

WOMAN: We don't have anything—

SWAGMAN: Not fussy about what it is—
WOMAN: Got nothing—
SWAGMAN: Must have a scrap or two around here—
WOMAN: I'm sorry—
SWAGMAN: What you feedin' that husband of yours, then?

Pause.

WOMAN: On account of the … sickness. His sickness. He's got no desire for food.
SWAGMAN: Don't sound like no man I ever met.
What's that?
WOMAN: Just some bread—old bread—
SWAGMAN: That'll do—
WOMAN: Saving it for—
SWAGMAN: Ya husband.
WOMAN: My husband.

Pause.

SWAGMAN: Won't mind, will he? Lackin' in hunger as he is.
WOMAN: For the moment.
SWAGMAN: Who knows how long?
Give us a bit.
WOMAN: Well—
If that'll help you on your way.
SWAGMAN: Most certainly will.

WOMAN *breaks off some bread and places it on the table.*

Grateful for your hospitality.

SWAGMAN *slowly walks over and picks up the bread.*

WOMAN: If you head along the river now, you'll make it to town before the sun goes down.
SWAGMAN: In no rush.

Pause.

Your husband awfully quiet.
Hearin' another man's voice coming' from his kitchen ought to cure him of whatever he got.
WOMAN: He's sleeping. Fever. Face like hot coals.

SWAGMAN: Reckon you better offer him somethin'.
WOMAN: He'll call out when he's got an appetite—
SWAGMAN: Sick man don't know himself.

Pause.

Take him the bread.
Stop me from eatin' the whole lot.
WOMAN: Might have trouble rousing him—
SWAGMAN: Give it a go.

WOMAN *hesitates.*

I'll watch over ya little one.

SWAGMAN *peers into the cradle.*

Like her old man?
WOMAN: Sorry?
SWAGMAN: Nothin' like you. Looks like your husband?
WOMAN: At first.

WOMAN *leaves quickly with the bread.*

SWAGMAN *listens intently.*

We see WOMAN *in the other room, coughing in the deepest voice she can muster.*

She quickly shoves pillows under a blanket, to give the impression of a someone lying in the bed.

There's silent panic in all of her movement.

[*Off*] No need to force it, my love.

WOMAN *coughs again.*

[*Off*] More rest will do you some good.

WOMAN *returns.*

SWAGMAN: A good woman, you are.
Can tell.
WOMAN: Glad you think so.

WOMAN *is becoming irritated.*

She notices SWAGMAN *is yet to finish his bread.*

If you ain't hungry, share with that poor mutt out there.

SWAGMAN: With him? Dog wants food, he'll find food.
WOMAN: Loyal dog worthy of a full belly too, ain't he?

Pause.

SWAGMAN: You're not wrong.

SWAGMAN *throws some bread out the door.*

We hear the scuffle and delight of the dog.

Noticed that fine-lookin' calf you got out there.
WOMAN: She's young. Been with me since birth.
SWAGMAN: And the cow?
WOMAN: Her mother is gone.
SWAGMAN: Gone?
WOMAN: That's right.
SWAGMAN: Not slaughtered for meat? Just *gone*?
WOMAN: Gone by my own hand.
SWAGMAN: Woman so fine?
WOMAN: Quicker than you think.
SWAGMAN: That so?
WOMAN: She came at me—great big cow—legs thicker than all your limbs put together. Huffing and snorting and building up to thumpin' into me.
But I got a knife.

WOMAN *picks up a knife from the kitchen table.*

She slowly walks towards SWAGMAN.

And I look her in the eyes—
And I stand my ground—
Don't let my hands shake or my eyes water up.
She gets closer—
And there's hate in her eyes—
Closer—
And there's power in her stride—
Closer—
Can almost feel her breath on my face—
Then she's there—
And I'm here—
And only one of us can win—
So I strike into her throat—

WOMAN *is very close to* SWAGMAN.

And blood pours out over my hands and she shrieks—
I see her eyes settle on her baby.
And I made a promise.
And I took in her girl.
I washed the blood off my hands—dipped them in the creek.
And I walked her home.

WOMAN *and* SWAGMAN *stare at each other.*

SWAGMAN *breaks away first.*

SWAGMAN: Your husband's got quite a woman on his hands.
He got a place to smoke? Away from your sweet baby?
WOMAN: Out the front, near the wood pile.
SWAGMAN: Excuse me for a moment.

SWAGMAN *pulls out his pipe and moves towards the door.*

WOMAN *is tense.*

SWAGMAN *opens the door.*

WOMAN *exhales slightly.*

Then—

SWAGMAN *swings around.*

Say—you got tobacco?
Sorry to ask so much of you—
Can't offer nothin' more than my thanks.
WOMAN: Tobacco?
I don't think—
We're out, I'm afraid.
SWAGMAN: Out? No tobacco for a smokin' man?

Silence.

WOMAN *and* SWAGMAN *lock eyes.*

WOMAN: Haven't been into town for a while.
He's been working.
SWAGMAN: He's been sick.
WOMAN: That's right.

Pause.

SWAGMAN: Well.

If there ain't no tobacco round here, I best be goin'.
Find myself a nice spot to spend the night.

Pause.

Give my regards to your husband.

SWAGMAN *departs, whistling to his dog.*

WOMAN *rushes to baby.*

WOMAN *holds baby tight.*

There's fear in the air.

She starts to barricade the house, pushing chairs up against the door.

WOMAN *is swallowed by the dark.*

SCENE TEN

GHOST *rocks baby.*

GHOST *follows something in the distance with her eyes.*

There's silence broken only by the sounds of crickets and swaying trees.

GHOST *places baby in the cradle.*

GHOST: The woman watches through the cracks, sees him wander off towards the sinking sun.

And then—

He turns around. Looks back at the house.

He stood like that for a while, pretendin' to fix up his swag. But she knew he was lookin'.

Then—

He moves towards the creek, which makes a bow around the house—

And she loses sight of him.

Pause.

Before night comes, she brings the calf in, closer than usual.

Strokes her head.

Puts food out on the front step, just out of her reach.

And beside it, lays down a string of shells.
Her mother's shells.
Only thing of value she's got.
She locks the doors.
Beside the bolt, she drives in a pair of scissors.
She piles the table and stools against it.
Tries to drink a cup of milk, but can't keep it down.
Hears the calf makin' a stir and shushes her up.
Only the baby seems calm.
Almost like she knows her mother don't have room in her brain or her heart for fussin'.
And then—
With no candle, no fire—
She creeps with the baby to bed.

GHOST *becomes* WOMAN.

WOMAN *holds baby close and falls asleep.*

Trees move.

Wind blows.

The house creeks.

Then—

A strange noise.

WOMAN *wakes.*

She's frozen.

SWAGMAN *is in the space.*

He's trying to find a way into the house.

SWAGMAN *moves around, testing entry points.*

WOMAN *creeps, barely breathing, trying to keep track of* SWAGMAN*'s whereabouts.*

SWAGMAN *sneaks,* WOMAN *hides.*

SWAGMAN *becomes more desperate—less careful.*

WOMAN *becomes more desperate—less hopeful.*

WOMAN *becomes* GHOST.

She thinks about trickin' him—about given' him an idea of where she might be—usin' her voice.
But her voice might wake the baby.
And so, she prays—somethin' she don't do usually.
Somethin' she learned.

Suddenly—

Baby stirs.

GHOST *becomes* WOMAN.

WOMAN: [*whispered*] No no no no no no.
Ssssshhhhhhh.
Please, baby.
Please, baby.
Ssssshhhhhhh.

Baby's cries become louder.

WOMAN *tries to silence baby.*

WOMAN *grabs a pillow and places it over the cradle.*

She presses down on the pillow.

Baby's cries are muffled.

WOMAN *is surprised and horrified by the impulse.*

WOMAN *throws the pillow aside, grabbing the screaming baby.*

SWAGMAN *springs into action, breaking into the house.*

Oh god oh god oh god oh god.

WOMAN *kicks down the door.*

She flees into the night.

SWAGMAN *stumbles into view.*

The chase begins.

SCENE ELEVEN

SWAGMAN *runs.*

GHOST *appears.*

GHOST: 'Oh god oh god oh god oh god—'
She thought—
She said—
She prayed—
Running out of the house—
Swagman tripping, giving her a moment—
And she runs past the calf—
Tethered to the post—
And she—
She goes back.
Unloops the rope.
'Run!'
Calf gets away faster than her and the baby—
They stumble—
Swagman was there, crouchin' down, outstretched arms.
She knew he was offerin' terms for stoppin' the struggle and cries for help.

Pause.

And it ain't till his hands grip my throat that the cries of—
MURDER—
MURDER—
Come from my lips.

Silence.

The startled crows took up the sound of my voice.
They went shriekin' over the Swagman's head.

Baby wails.

Darkness.

SCENE TWELVE

The faint galloping of a horse.

HORSEMAN *appears.*

HORSEMAN: Father, what I saw was—
Well, a horseman like me ain't never seen something so—
Well—
There ain't words.
When ya see something like—
Somethin' so—
To say it—with *words*—means to … make it small.
Diminish? That the word?
Talkin' like a fool—
Like a man in love.

Pause.

I was ridin' into town after vistin' the old lady. She lives on her own way out bush. Gets no trouble. Minds her own business. But can talk the balls off a bull, that's for sure. So I was stuck there till late, so I spent the night, sleepin' on a mat out on the front porch. Hate the indoors. Hate bein' covered up.

And I wake—and the day feels different to other days and the trees stand different to other days. There's somethin' … *new* about the dawn and the sun doesn't burn my neck so much. My horse feels different and we're gliding—fuckin' gliding—across ground that usually causes me to thump against her back, fearin' I'll crack her spine. We pass a calf, grazing. An old wine shanty, door hanging open. And the air feels … light. Clear as the river. Slips into my lungs in a way it never has before.

And then—
I see her.
Near the river.
Crinkled clothes and tangled black hair was all I could make out.
And I don't dare step down from my horse—
Because I see—

GHOST *appears.*

GHOST: You see?

HORSEMAN: A beautiful woman—

GHOST: You see a woman—

HORSEMAN: Peaceful face—

GHOST: Brown eyes agape, mouth loose, nose dripping—

HORSEMAN: Lips pink—

GHOST: Lips bloodied and bulging—

HORSEMAN: Head tilted—

GHOST: Twisted—

HORSEMAN: Like she drifted off in a daydream—

GHOST: Like she had a scream in her throat—

HORSEMAN: Skin—

GHOST: Black as night—

HORSEMAN: Caramel—

GHOST: Sweat from panic—

HORSEMAN: Laid out like a piece of fuckin' silk—

GHOST: Like a rag—

HORSEMAN: Palms turned up—

GHOST: Nails blunt—

HORSEMAN: Fingers stretched out—

GHOST: Knuckles scuffed like bark on a tree—

HORSEMAN: Hair mussed up with leaves from a—

GHOST: With sticks from the ground—

HORSEMAN: Arranged just so—

GHOST: Like daggers to her scalp—

HORSEMAN: And then—

GHOST: And then—

HORSEMAN: The thing that made me shiver—

GHOST: That made you wish—

HORSEMAN: Clinging to this woman—

GHOST: Feeding off this woman—

HORSEMAN: A baby, suckling from her breast. Peaceful, like her, drinking in life. Eyes closed, too, soft hands against soft skin, hunger on its lips—

GHOST: The girl's lips—

HORSEMAN: The baby—

GHOST: A girl—
HORSEMAN: Didn't notice me approaching, even upon a horse.
GHOST: Too hungry to notice—
HORSEMAN: And what I saw, Father—
There in the dirt and not three metres from the river—

Pause.

The Virgin Mary.
GHOST: She's no virgin—
No divine wisdom written across her face—
No trip to heaven ahead of her.
She's a woman far from home, layin' still in the dirt—
Dirt that will take her back.
HORSEMAN: That's why I came, Father.
Because—
And I swear it now, right in front of you—
I saw Her.
GHOST: You saw her.
Her and *her*.
Mother and baby.
Baby too tired—
Baby too hungry—
To give you a glance.
And woman too dead.
Life flowing from her still, though her heart stopped and her hand's cold.
HORSEMAN: I don't reach out for the baby.
Don't stroke the woman's hair or feel her neck for a pulse—
GHOST: The dead can see too, you know.
I see my baby and I see her sucking even though I can't feel nothin'. And I will my arms to move and hold her close and adjust her latch and give her what she needs, but I just lay there, still as a log.
And as my eyes start to go black—when the horseman's face gets blurred and the legs of his horse tramp off across the river—
I think only of her and her hungry belly.
HORSEMAN: So, Father, I rode out to tell you—
What I saw.

HORSEMAN *falls to his knees in prayer.*

GHOST: If the dead can see, why can't you?

GHOST *disappears.*

SCENE THIRTEEN

The click-clack of shoes.

Then—

PRIEST *appears.*

He's got an accent of some kind—

Irish or Scottish or English or something like that.

He's got authority.

He's charismatic.

He speaks to the audience.

PRIEST: Seen it with your own eyes, eh?
God's eyes?
The Horseman came to me with a vision—
I would not give his state of fancy more weight than that—
Of a woman.
Riding into town, upon his horse, he saw her.
And he stopped by her.
And noticed her whimpering baby.
And this vision led to a realisation.
Of beauty? Of this cracked glass we call life? The power of our brains to see what we want?

Pause.

There's no man—white collar or none—Jesuit or otherwise—who hasn't seen a woman, lying in nature, soft skin resting on green grass.
Man is made to see such things. To *want* such things.

Pause.

The Virgin Mary appeared to me as a boy.

I played in the field, under peach trees. I could see my mother through the kitchen window. My siblings rested on flat stones dug up from the property.

And during my games—I saw a woman in a tree, balanced on the branches. And I saw her breasts, full. And I saw her palms turned up to the clouds, and I saw the half-smile on her face. Skin like snow.

And I told my brother and my sister about this woman. And they couldn't see what I saw.

And I told my mother about the woman. And she dropped the bowl in her hands and crumpled to her knees and spoke to Mary—

'For the love of Christ, save him!'

The grief in her face made me tremble.

My lord and god—thou hast chosen me?

And my path was set.

Pause.

What do you make of the Horseman's vision?

A white-robed figure, clasping a baby, resting on a patch of pipe-clay by the river? The moonlight on the clay crowned her head in blue.

Flesh and blood? Or heavenly creature?

And the woman's …

Complexion.

Not white—not pale.

Kissed by night.

And the baby—

Cheeks marked with the colour of dusk.

Sure to blacken up—if only slightly.

And this cannot be salvation—a woman like this.

And her baby cannot be our saviour.

'You shalt not sow your fields with two kinds of seed.'

Black and white.

'As you sow the iron mud with soft clay, so they will mix with one another in marriage, but they will not hold together, just as iron does not mix with clay.'

Pause.

What I said to the Horseman, I will say again now:

I have walked with these people—

Jesuits have walked for some time now—

With these people.

There has been dialogue.
Both ways.
And we have told them of the mercy and salvation that awaits—
If only they look up—
If only they put their faith in something more tangible—
Than sky and sea.
But not all men are created equal nor are they viewed as equal in the eyes of God when he is wilfully ignored.
And some of these—
These people—
Who do not learn about Cain and Abel—
Who do not *know* Mary—as she exists on the page and in the minds of our brotherhood—and the love and forgiveness that sits within her heart and soul—
Will only know a fraction of what life can be.
And their death will be an eternity in the making.

Pause.

We came here to help.
To spread teachings—
God's word.
Jesus' love.

GHOST *appears with baby.*

She gives the impression of the Virgin Mary—maybe with her clothes or a ring of light around her head.

The Horseman saw nothing that day.
A glimmer of white. A smear of black.
Whining of a calf from somewhere far off.
And his loosened tongue poured out a warning.

PRIEST *approaches* GHOST.

PRIEST *takes baby and rocks it in his arms.*

GHOST *turns to the audience.*

GHOST: You die in a bed.
Head restin' on somethin' soft—
Bright light—

White light—

White sheets pressed up against ya white skin.

Breath comin' slow and steady—

Hand of ya children, hand of your friend, hand of a woman in white who done this before—

Skin on skin—but the wanted kind—

The gentle kind.

You gone without fuss.

You gone wrapped up in—

Wrapped up in—

Love.

Pause.

Many miles down the creek, a man throws stones into a waterhole. He dips his knife in the water and it washes off pink.

Pause.

If the dead can see, why can't you?

Baby cries.

GHOST *hangs a string of shells around baby's neck.*

GHOST *disappears.*

Sounds of the river.

Blackout.

THE END

THE STREET PRESENTS

THE CHOSEN VESSEL

BY DYLAN VAN DEN BERG

AFTER THE SHORT STORY BY BARBARA BAYNTON

World Premiere Season at The Street Theatre, Canberra
09–24 August 2025

The Chosen Vessel was first imagined and incubated through The Street Theatre's concept development program **Early Phase** in 2020. Subsequently in 2021, The Street Theatre commissioned Dylan Van Den Berg to write the adaptation. Creative development was through our First Seen program, with playwright Dylan supported in this development by the Rodney Seaborn Playwright's Trust.

GOVERNMENT ACKNOWLEDGEMENTS
This project is made possible with the support of the ACT government

THE STREET COMPANY

Artistic Director and CEO	Caroline Stacey OAM
Executive Producer	Dean Ellis
Technical Manager	Neil Simpson
Front of House Manager	Pierce Craswell
Communications - Publicity	Su Hodge
Front of House	Lauren Crean, Pierce Craswell , Eloise Kenny, Elio Robertson
Design and Artwork	Tobi Skerra

THE STREET BOARD

We acknowledge the Ngunnawal and Ngambri peoples as the Traditional Owners of the unceded lands on which The Street Theatre stands and where we work, create, gather and live. We recognise their continuing connection to land, waters, community and culture, and pay our respects to their Elders past and present.

The Street is an ACT Government Arts Centre managed by The Stagemaster Inc., a not-for-profit organisation. The Street is supported by the ACT Government through artsACT.

CAST

In order of appearance

Laila Thaker

Craig Alexander

CREATIVE TEAM

Direction	Abbie-lee Lewis
Set Design	Angie Matsinos
Costume Design	Leah Ridley
Lighting Design	Nathan Sciberras
Sound Design	Kyle Sheedy

PRODUCTION TEAM

Stage Manager	Zsuzsi Soboslay
Lighting Operator	Emma Burrows
Sound Operator	Kyle Sheedy
Set Construction	Bret Ridley, Irwin Ross
Stage Technicians	Connor McKay, Wayne Bateup
Artwork	Tobi Skerra
Photography	Novel Photographic, Nathan Smith Photography
Videography	Craig Alexander, Shelly Higgs
Rehearsal Observation	Fi Peel

SETTING

The action of *The Chosen Vessel* takes place in the early 1900s in various locations including: a small house in the middle of the bush, a whitefella house in town, a pub and a spirit-world.

WRITER'S NOTE

The Chosen Vessel began as a conversation with a colonial ghost – Barbara Baynton's 19th-century short story of the same name. I was struck by it as a feminist response to Henry Lawson's *The Drover's Wife*, by Baynton's refusal to skirt around the edges of male violence, by her evocative depiction of what it was to be a mother isolated in the bush. It's a story rich with zigs and zags for interpretation, reimaginings and – at times – contestation.

Adaptation comes with a series of responsibilities: to the original work, to yourself and what you'd like to say, to the people who love and expect certain things from the original. The biggest challenge is balancing these things and still saying something new – in ways that dawn gradually or perhaps even explosively.

In Baynton's original, a white woman and her baby are attacked in the bush, their violent experience re-cast by men as a parable of Christian sacrifice. That transformation – from life into myth – is where my version of the story sits: in positioning a Blak woman at the centre, who gets to tell the story of her life and death? Who gets to ink the pages of history? For First Nations peoples, personal narratives have always collided with the dominant story of 'Australia', the lived realities of our lives often erased.

Blackfellas in early literature were either non-existent or present only in the margins of a work – mystical spectres, fodder for violence, rarely given full and complex lives on the page or the stage. The woman at the centre of this play is not just a victim of violence; she is a dreamer, a daughter, a mother, and – crucially – a storyteller in her own right.

This work wrestles with the form of the Aboriginal Gothic, a genre where haunting and history are inseparable, where its stock features are not merely elements of fearful fancy but grounded firmly in reality. In the Aboriginal Gothic, Country is not a blank or alien landscape to be conquered, as in settler narratives of the last two centuries, but a place of connection and comfort. Haunting of Country is a mechanism for truth-telling, a way for the past to assert itself when it has been denied.

This is a play that sits in discomfort, where stories collide and overwrite one another. Thank you for sitting with the silences in our nation's history, and for being a part of re-writing the story.

Dylan Van Den Berg
July 2025, Ngunnawal and Ngambri Country

THE ABORIGINAL GOTHIC

The term *Aboriginal Gothic* is a contested one – and for good reason. The Gothic tradition itself carries colonial baggage, and there are legitimate concerns about the misrepresentation and exploitation of Aboriginal and Torres Strait Islander peoples when their stories are filtered through a genre historically shaped by European anxieties.

But First Nations writers and artists have not simply inherited the Gothic; we have *commandeered* it. In doing so, we exercise self-determination, transforming the genre into a mode of creative resistance. This adaptation is not passive: it is deliberate, creating space for First Nations artists to attend to cultural experiences, grapple with a bloody national history, and assert our own truths about this country's foundations.

Where the Australian Gothic often depicts settler unease in an unfamiliar and threatening landscape, the Aboriginal Gothic reflects something very different: a First Nations unease not with the land itself, but with how it has been irrevocably transformed by colonisation. Here, the land is not alien but familiar and intimate: it bears witness to colonial violence, dispossession, and trauma, and the haunting emerges from that rupture.

Features of the Aboriginal Gothic include a dislocation of time, where terror and history collapse into one another, and an absence of the tidy restoration of order that defines traditional European Gothic narratives. There are no neat endings here, no easy return to safety. Instead, these works dwell in the intersection of past, present, and future, refusing to separate history from 'now'.

In the hands of Aboriginal and Torres Strait Islander artists, the Gothic becomes a tool for revising colonial encounters and reasserting Blak identity/ies. The Aboriginal Gothic is comfortable with shadows. It is a place where history is unmade and remade, where the atrocities of the past are not buried but carried forward, part of the present, inescapable and unfinished.

If this land, This Country could speak what would it say? How would it say it?

It takes a lot for our people to continuously be reminded of the violence inflicted on us in this society and yet it is necessary for us to continue to tell the hard truths of this country's history in hopes that the rest of this country can reckon with its past.

On first reading Dylan's adaptation of *The Chosen Vessel* I was struck by its boldness in highlighting the harsh realities that indigenous women would have had to endure post colonial invasion. It's a work that doesn't shy away from the cruelty of that world whilst still managing to express the resilience and strength that lives in all First Nation people. In the past few years as I have moved from being an actor into directing I have been driven by a need to tell our stories our way. It is my belief that how we make our stories and deliver them is just as important as the stories themselves as it is an extension of our culture. Live story telling is our education and so the craft of telling them needs just as much thought as the stories we write and tell. So often western theatrical craft is about who has the power to tell stories, what stories are historized and who historicized them. Whose writing and stories is deemed Important and to whom in what context. I wanted to use the offer of the Aboriginal Gothic genre this piece grapples with as a way to explore this work safely to those whose role it is to bring this work to life and to those who witness it. By leaning on the genre of the work I hope to be able to highlight the works themes by basing them in reality but delivering them in a stylised form. The genre forces audiences to digest hard truths without shying away from reality,in turn allowing them to grapple with this country's grim history.

Abbie-lee Lewis
July 2025, Ngunnawal and Ngambri Country

BARBARA BAYNTON
Author

Barbara Baynton (1857–1929) was born in the Hunter Valley town of Scone, New South Wales. She was an Australian author of the same period as Henry Lawson – the Bush Realism school of the 1890s fostered by the Sydney Bulletin. In the 1890s, she began writing short stories, poetry and articles for the Bulletin, where *The Chosen Vessel* was first published as *The Tramp* in 1896. Her collection of six short stories, *Bush Studies*, was published in Duckworth in 1902 and is famous for not romanticising bush life, instead showing all its bleakness and harshness. Economic of style, influenced by the great nineteenth-century Russian novelists, Baynton presents the Australian bush as dangerous and isolating for the women who inhabit it. **Bush Studies** is published by Text Classics with an introduction by Helen Garner.

https://bookanista.com/chosen-vessel/

DYLAN VAN DEN BERG
Playwright

Dylan Van Den Berg is a Palawa writer and dramaturg from the northeast of Lutruwita/Tasmania, with family connections to the Bass Strait Islands where his great-grandmother was born. As a playwright, recent credits include: *Whitefella Yella Tree* (Griffin Theatre Company/ Sydney Theatre Company/La Boite; *Milk*; *The Chosen Vessel* (The Street Theatre); *Way Back When* (The Old Fitz); *All that Glitters is Not Mould* (National Institute of Dramatic Art); *Ngadjung* (Belco Arts); *The Camel* (FlickFlick City/Motley Bauhaus). For screen, Dylan has written extensively for Play School (ABC) and has joined writers' rooms for Blackfella Films, Wooden Horse, and Warner Bros.

Dylan was awarded his second Rodney Seaborn Playwright Award in 2022 for *The Chosen Vessel*. Other awards for his writing and plays include: the Griffin Award; two AWGIES; the David Williamson Prize; Kate Challis RAKA Award; two NSW Premier's Literary Awards for Playwriting; the Victorian Premier's Literary Award for Drama; and, Australian Theatre Festival NYC 2025 New Play Award. He was shortlisted for the Bruntwood International Playwriting Prize. He is currently under commission with Griffin Theatre Company and Malthouse Theatre. Dylan studied drama at the ANU and is undertaking a PhD in Aboriginal Gothic Theatre at the University of Canberra.

ABBIE-LEE LEWIS
Director

Abbie-lee Lewis is a Kalkadoon actor and director who trained in the Aboriginal Theatre and Acting courses at the Western Australian Academy of Performing Arts, Perth. In 2022 she made her directing debut with Bruce Pascoe's *Cutter and Coot* (Moogahlin Performing Arts) and has since directed *An Ox Stand On My Tongue* by Jane Montgomery Griffith (Belvoir 25A) and *Saplings* by Hannah Belanszky (Australian Theatre for Young People) which received a Sydney Theatre Award for best production for young people. Her debut play *Dirty Diamonds* was a finalist for the Australian Theatre Festival of NYC 2025 New Play Award.

She has worked as an assistant director on *Hamlet* and *Macbeth* (Bell Shakespeare). Abbie-lee was the recipient of the 2022 Andrew Cameron fellowship with Belvoir, assisting Sarah Goodes on *The Weekend.* Television credits include *Black Comedy* (ABC).

Recent actor stage credits include: *Counting and Cracking*, *Scenes from the Climate Era* (Belvoir); *Our Town* (Black Swan State Theatre Company); *A Midsummer Night's Dream* (Bell Shakespeare); *The Bleeding Tree* (Blue Room Theatre, Perth); and *Fallen* (Sport for Jove).

CRAIG ALEXANDER
Actor

Craig Alexander is an award-winning Australian actor, writer, and filmmaker known for his ability to blend comedy and tragedy alongside his diverse range of creative abilities. Armed with a B.A. (Honours) in Acting from CSU, Craig has been a prominent figure in the theatre industry for nearly two decades. However, his recent focus has shifted toward captivating screen content, working both in front of and behind the camera. Recent stage performance credits include: *Waiting for Godot*, *Art*, *St Nicholas*, *Venus in Fur* (The Street); *Unprecedented* (Hothouse Theatre); *Just Hearing* (REBUS Theatre); and *Wolf Lullaby* (Echo Theatre).

Recent screen performance credits include: *The Silent Service* (Amazon), *Murder In The Outback* (Channel 7/Beyond), *Invited* (Berger-Alexander, Best Actor CSFF 2021), *The Photographer* (thehorse.media, Best Actor CSFF 2019) *Dirt* (Next In Line Films, Best Actor Fleurieue Film Fest 2018). He recently completed his first Feature *Snatchers*, which premiered at Raindance Film Festival and is due for release in Australia later this year.

LAILA THAKER
Actor

Laila Thaker is a staunch Torres Strait Islander (Meriam/Wagadagam) and Indian (Ratlamwali) actor. Since graduating with a BA in Theatre (JCU Cairns) and Cert IV in Film and Television (TAW Brisbane), she has been cast in various roles from Shakespeare to Sarah Kane.

Her stage credits include: *Super* (Red Stitch Theatre) *The Return* (Malthouse Theatre), *Coconut Woman* (YIRRAMBOI), *Viral* (ILBIJERRI). Screen crediits include: *RFDS* (Channel 7), *Apple Cider Vinegar* (Netflix), *Five Bedrooms* (Paramount), *Wentworth* (Foxtel), *Informer 3838* (Nine Network), *My Life is Murder* (Channel Ten), *Bad Mothers* (Nine Network), *The Queen and I* (NITV/ABC), *House Husbands* (Nine Network) and LA feature films *San Andreas* and *Christmas Downunder*. Her role in *Prayers to Broken Stone* (Boutique Theatre) won her Best Emerging Indigenous Artist for the Melbourne Fringe Awards (2017). As a member of ICMEAA, Laila continues to empower First Nations voices and affirm Blak storytelling that's meaningful in the arts.

ANGIE MATSINOS
Set Design

Angie Matsinos has worked in set, costume, and prop design for stage productions, large-scale events, and television. Professional theatre credits include set and costume design: for *Cho Doi* (Market of Lives) by Dinh Thi Nguyen, *The Beggars Opera* by John Gay (Bridge Theatre, Wollongong); *Undiscovered Country* by Vanessa Badham (Hope Theatre, Wollongong). She was part of the Sydney 2000 Olympic Games Opening Ceremony design team, working under Donny Woolagoodja and Peter England to create the giant Namarali Wandjina. Television credits include: *Hi-5* (ABC/Channel Nine). Other creative work includes: Darwin Fringe Festival site dressing; and the Weereewa Festival, a site-specific installation design for the Mirramu Dance Company's production of *Silk* on the shores of Lake George.

Awards include: the Sydney Morning Herald On This Day Art Award; multiple *Gould League Art Awards* for illustration; *Design-Tech* Powerhouse Museum exhibition for set and costume design of Macbeth, and a costume design featured in Centre-staged Fringe Fashion Showcase Melbourne. She holds a Bachelor of Creative Arts (Theatre Design) from the University of Wollongong, where studies encompassed design realisation, dramaturgy, and visual arts.

LEAH RIDLEY
Costume Design

Leah Ridley is a costume designer and textile artist based in Canberra. Costume design and credits include: *Utopiate* (Rebus Theatre); and, *Eurydice* (Mill Theatre). In 2023 she designed and created the robot costume for the roving performer 'Wheely Wonky'. Completing a Diploma of Fashion Design and a Diploma of Costume for Performance at Wollongbar TAFE in 2022, she returned to Canberra after her studies.

NATHAN SCIBERRAS
Lighting Design

Nathan Sciberras has worked across numerous roles in the arts: lighting designer, event manager for live events and major festivals, a theatrical and concert, musician, conductor, musical director and arts educator. He has worked with The Street on numerous music performances and also designed for the Canberra International Music Festival. Theatre Lighting design credits include: *Who's Afraid of Virginia Woolf*; *Hand to God*; and, *Holding the Man* (ACT Hub); *Waiting in the Wings* (The Q); *Rope*; *What the Butler Saw* (CAT Awards for lighting design in 2020 and 2021); and the world premiere of *Baby Jane* (Canberra Rep). Away from the theatre, Nathan is also a musician, playing in the Canberra group **Brass Knuckle Brass Band**.

KYLE SHEEDY
Sound Design

Kyle Sheedy is an Audio Engineer based in Canberra who began working in theatre as a general technician and operator. Sound design credits include *This Rough Magic*; *Constellations*; *Tourmaline, The War of The Worlds*; *Venus in Fur*; *Fragments*; *A Doll's House, Part 2* (The Street Theatre). He also has worked as an Audio Operator on The Street Theatre productions: *The Faithful Servant*; *Cold Light*; *Boys Will Be Boys*. Other productions include: *Urinetown*, *The Hello Girls* (Heart Strings Theatre Co); *Mess*; *Intimacy* (Belconnen Arts centre); *Drought and Other Plays* by Millicent Armstrong (Music Theatre Projects Ltd). He obtained an Advanced Diploma in Sound Production through CIT.

ZSUZSI SOBOSLAY
Stage Manager

Zsuzsi Soboslay has worked in various capacities in association with The Street Theatre as actor, writer, director, movement consultant [*The Chain Bridge*, *Anthems and Angels*, *The Story of the Oars*, *Cold Light*], as stage manager for *The Maids* and in various script developments.

She created *L'Optimisme on the life of Jane Avril*, muse to Toulouse Lautrec [NGA Enlighten], *The Compassion Plays* [Gorman Arts Centre,] on refugee experience; and *The Culture Hub* and *Moon Stories*, as culturally-diverse, intergenerational, multidisciplinary works developed in community.

Films include *Snatchers* [The Horse Media] and the Lea/Nugent/Healy award-winning dance-on-film *And....Breathe*. In 2020, in partnership with The Street she created *ReStorying*, an online resource project to help replenish artists affected by Covid-19. She is currently developing a multi-artform story exchange and podcast program, *The Story Chapel*, focussed on underrepresented voices including the experience of those working with birth, death and in transitions

ABOUT THE STREET

Inquiry and Imagination

The Street Theatre is Canberra's creative powerhouse of inquiry, ideas and imagination. A theatre of new and old work where big ideas are sparked and shared. A place for everyone to engage in dialogue, explore new artistic expressions, and witness the city's creative energy at its best.

The Street commissions, develops, produces and presents live performance that helps us talk to who we are and the world around us. We are Canberra's award-winning major investor in new theatre, music, comedy and multi-artform work employing some of the finest artists, makers, and technicians in the region and diaspora over the last two decades.

Just as Canberra is considered a petri-dish for new policies, ideas and cultural products within the broader national landscape, The Street serves a vital role as a key creative generator of new work and regenerator of place and community within the nation's political heart.

The Street believes in the remarkable capacity of Canberra artists to create experiences that resonate deeply and expand perspectives by blending vision, ambition, and creativity with thought-provoking ideas.

The Street was the recipient of the 2020 Sidney Myer Performing Arts Award for outstanding achievement and is an essential contributor to the well-being of residents in the ACT and artistic vibrancy in the region.

WWW.THESTREET.ORG.AU

FIND US

Phone (02) 6247 1223

Address 15 Childers Street
Canberra City

Social #thestreetcbr
#thestreetART
@thestreetcbr

Supported by

The Street is managed by The Stagemaster Inc., a not-for-profit organisation. The Street is supported by the ACT government through artsACT and is an ACT Government Arts Centre.

PRODUCTION SPONSOR

We thank our Street Supporters for their donations supporting bringing *The Chosen Vessel* to the stage.

WWW.THESTREET.ORG.AU/SUPPORT-US/OUR-SUPPORTERS

ACKNOWLEDGEMENTS

From The Street

We thank the following people for their generous creative contribution to the development of *The Chosen Vessel*: 2020 Early Phasers – Adam Broinowski, Linda Chen, Sally Marrett, Jo Richards, Ylaria Rogers, Kenneth Spiteri; actors Angeline Penrith and Craig Alexander; designer Imogen Keen; director Abbie-lee Lewis.

From The PlayWright DYLAN VAN DEN BERG

This work was conceived as part of The Street's Early Phase Program, and further developed through the First Seen initiative. It was commissioned, produced and published by The Street. The author wishes to express deep gratitude for the ongoing support of The Street, the ACT's premier producer of new work.

The author is indebted to the following people for their advice and creative wisdom along the way: Associate Professor Jen Crawford, Dr Paul Collis, Professor Paul Magee, Tiannah Van Den Berg, Emily Clark, Angus Cerini, Nicola Darcy, Hannah Wood, Peter Matheson, Dr Rebecca Clode, Caroline Stacey OAM and Shelly Higgs.

THE STREET DONORS

STREET-LIGHT(20,000+)
Carey Gaul

STREET-LIFE ($5,000+)
Michael Adena and Joanne Daly, Cathy Winters

STREET-PARTY ($1,000+)
Joan Adler, Raoul Craemer, Colin Neave AM, Michael Sassella, Caroline Stacey OAM, David Williams AM, Secret Admirers (2)

STREET-WORKS ($500+)
John Addis, Peta Spender, Peter Wise, Secret Admirers (2)

STREET-STYLE ($250+)
Dr Barrie Stacey, Adam Stankevicius, Secret Admirers (3)

STREET-WISE (UP TO $250)
Margaret Adamson, Janet Aitken, Sandra Aldridge, Chris & Angelika Ansted & Dunker, Susan Archer, Louise Armstrong, Vickie Bennett, Neville Bleakley, Zel Bodulovic, Tim Bowyer, Sarah Brasch, Karlie Brown, Kaye Browning, Penny Calvert, Helen Catchatoor, Sally Catchpole, Anne Cawsey, Mary Chapman, William Christie, Marie Cifuentes, Andrea Close, Patrice Coffee, Kylie Coghill, Ash Collins, Jennifer Coulston, Peter Cranston, Heather Crawford, Teresa Crowley, Michelle Curry, Caroline Dawson, Genevieve Derwent, Ilona DiBella, Dominique Doyle, Kym Duggan, Tracey Duren, Sue Dyer, Gerard Early, Amy Fahey, Becky Flores, Michael Foley, Ron Fraser, Toni French, Sheila Garrett, Louise Gell, Nick George, Jacinta George, Mark Gibbons, Lynne Gillam, Ross Girvan, Martin Glover, Julian Goldenberg, Luis Gómez Romero, Martha Grahme, Brendan Greenhill, Karen Groeneveld, Ian Hallet, Stuart Hamilton, Bronwyn Hatherly, Thomas Joseph Higgins, Meredith Hinchliffe, Su Hodge, Barbara Holloway, Lauren Honcope, Luke Horne, Philippa Horner, Jeffrey Ibbotson, Dee Jago, Gary James, Mary Jordan, Robyn Kelly, Rob Kennedy, Evan Kidd, Giselle Lamberth, Jonathon A Lane, Steve Le Lievre, Anthony Leake, Fleur Leary, Michele Legge, Henry Lis, Dianne Lucas, Paul Lynch, Charles Macleod, Sharyn Madigan, Sally Mansfield, Simon Marrable, Julia Martin, Rodney Maxted, Barbara McCauley, Fergus McCowan, Craig McDonald, Terry McDonald, Jane McGauley, Chirstopher McLeod, Maria Meere, Will Middleton, Margaret Millard, Simon Mitchell, Lavinia Mitchell, Craig Muller, Simon Murnane, Amanda O'Neill, Glenn O'Sullivan, Valia Palmer, Nicholas Pardy, Maddi Parker, Simi Parker, Deb Phillips, Deb Pippen, Andrew Purdham, Daniel Radford, Denise Rawling, Gill Reeves, Lynlea Rodger, David Roland, Linda Rossiter, Catherine Rumble, Steve Scul, Agneta Sherborne, Robert Slape, Michael Smith, Sam Smith, Helen Smith, David Stanton, Alan Stephens, Jessica Sutherland, Peta Swarbrick, Julia Taylor, Catherine Taylor, Sally Troy, Andrea Twell, Jocelyn Vasey, Lee-Anne Vickers, Sarah White, Rosemary White, Anne Williams, Lyn Witheridge, Audrey Young, Secret Admirers.